SUDAN

MAJOR WORLD NATIONS

SUDAN

Ingrid and Miles Roddis

CHELSEA HOUSE PUBLISHERS
Philadelphia

Chelsea House Publishers

http://www.chelseahouse.com

Copyright © 2000, 2001 by Chelsea House Publishers,
a subsidiary of Haights Cross Communications.
All rights reserved.
Printed in Malaysia

3 5 7 9 8 6 4

Library of Congress Cataloging-in-Publication Data

Roddis, Ingrid.
Sudan / Ingrid and Miles Roddis.
p.   cm. — (Major world nations)
Includes index.
Summary: Surveys the history, topography, government, people, and culture
of Sudan.
ISBN 0-7910-5398-9 (hc.)
1. Sudan—Juvenile literature. [1. Sudan.]   I. Roddis, Miles.
II. Roddis, Ingrid. Let's visit Sudan. III. Title. IV. Series.
DT154.6.R63   1999
962.4—dc21   99-11831
CIP

CONTENTS

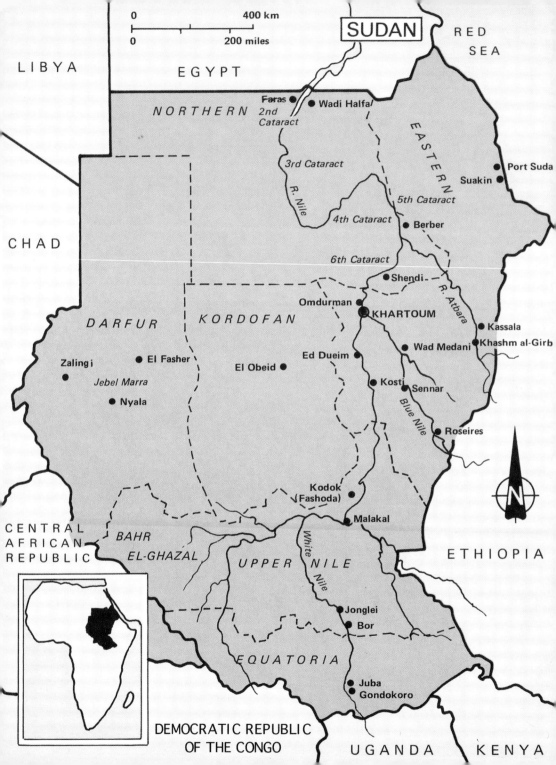

FACTS AT A GLANCE

Land and People

Official Name	Republic of Sudan
Location	Northern Africa
Area	1,000,000 square miles (2,505,810 square kilometers)
Climate	Tropical
Capital	Khartoum
Other Cities	Juba, Nyala, Port Sudan
Population	33,500,000
Population Distribution	Urban, 24.6 percent; rural 75.4 percent
Major Rivers	White Nile, Blue Nile
Major Lakes	Nubia
Mountains	Jebel Marra
Official Language	Arabic
Other Languages	English, Nubian, various dialects

Ethnic Groups	Black, 52 percent; Arab, 39 percent
Religions	Sunni Muslim, 70 percent; indigenous beliefs, 25 percent
Literacy Rate	46 percent
Average Life Expectancy	55.97

Economy

Natural Resources	Petroleum
Division of Labor Force	Agriculture, 80 percent; industry and commerce, 10 percent
Agricultural Products	Cotton, peanuts (groundnuts), millet, wheat, sesame seeds, citrus fruits, dates
Industries	Cotton, textiles, edible oils
Major Imports	Food, petroleum products, machinery, medicines and chemicals, manufactured goods
Major Exports	Cotton, sesame, livestock
Major Trading Partners	Saudi Arabia, European Union, China, Egypt
Currency	Sudanese pound

Government

Form of Government	Transitional (from military regime)
Government Bodies	National Assembly
Formal Head of State	President

HISTORY AT A GLANCE

590 B.C.-350 A.D.	The Meroitic civilization thrives at the triangle between the Atbara and Nile rivers.
350 A.D.	The city of Meroe is destroyed by the Ethiopians.
4th century	Three Christian kingdoms arise in the area–Nobatia, Makurra, and Alwa.
641 A.D.	Arabs bring the Islamic religion to the area and the Muslims and Christians sign a treaty agreeing to live peacefully with each other.
7th-14th centuries	The Christian kingdoms gradually die out and the area becomes predominantly Muslim. Increasing numbers of Arabs settle in the area.
1504	A group called the Funj move into the area and rule for almost 300 years.
18th-19th centuries	The slave trade increases in the area and some of the weaker tribes are nearly wiped out.
1820	Egypt, as a province of the Ottoman Empire, invades the Sudan and rules for the next 60 years.
1839	A Turkish sailor, Captain Salim, explores the upper White Nile. Agriculture is improved and more crops are grown.

9

1881-1898	This time is referred to as the Mahdiya in Sudan because it marks the rule of Muhammed Ahmed, the Mahdi, and his successor, Khalifa Abdullahi.
1883	At the battle of Shaykan, the Mahdi's followers defeat 10,000 Egyptian troops under British command. The Mahdi's troops continue to be victorious all over northern Africa.
1885	Khartoum comes under siege by the Mahdi's troops and falls, with most of the British and Egyptian troops killed. Mahdi dies and is succeeded by Khalifa Abdullahi.
1885-1890	Sudan suffers years of famine and a small pox epidemic.
1898	The British and Egyptian troops under Herbert Kitchener invade the Sudan. At the battle of Omdurman the Anglo-Egyptians are victorious and rule the area until 1956.
1906	Port Sudan is constructed and becomes Sudan's only major port.
early 20th century	Efforts to stop the slave trade finally make headway and it gradually comes to an end.
1922	The British make the southern regions of Sudan a "closed district" separating them from the north to try to retain some of the south's cultures.
1926	The Gezira Scheme is opened, the world's largest cooperative farming project for the production of cotton.
1940s	Various groups rise up in the Sudan and begin to work for independence.
1953	An Anglo-Egyptian agreement is signed agreeing to a three-year preparation for independence.

1956	January 1st Sudan officially becomes an independent nation.
1956-1958	The government changes numerous times. The country experiences two years of bad cotton harvests. Civil war in the south which had been festering for years continues.
1958	Under General Ibrahim Abboud the military takes control of the government. All political parties and trade unions are banned.
1964	General Abboud is forced to resign and parliamentary rule returns. The civil war in the south continues.
1969	Again the military takes over the government, this time under the leadership of Jaafar Nimeiri.
1970s	Under Nimeiri's rule roads are expanded, an oil pipeline is laid, agricultural projects are financed, and the foreign debts grow.
1972	The Addis Ababa Peace Agreement is signed with the southern rebels making a separate Southern Region. Peace in the south allows for some improvements in the infrastructure.
1984	Over one million refugees come to Sudan fleeing wars and drought in Ethiopia and Chad. This puts a strain on Sudan's already depleted resources.
1985	Nimeiri dissolves the separate southern region, introduces harsh interpretations of Islamic law. He is overthrown by the army which promises elections in the next year.
1989	The Revolutionary Command Council (RCC), led by General al-Bashir, seizes power and with great ruthlessness takes over control of all aspects of Sudanese life.

1991 The military government supports Iraq in the Persian Gulf War alienating Western countries and some Arab countries as well. The southern Sudanese People's Liberation Army (SPLA) continues its fight with war, famine, and drought spreading through the southern regions.

1992 The United Nations General Assembly passes a resolution expressing deep concern over human rights violations in Sudan.

1993 The military government disbands and appoints General Bashir as president.

1994 The government launches a large-scale attack against the southern rebels cutting off relief aid coming from Kenya and Uganda. Thousands of refugees flee.

1996 Sudan's government is crippled by foreign debt. The first elections are held since 1989. Hassan at-Turabi is elected president. A peace treaty is signed with two rebel groups in the south but the SPLA continues its fight.

1997 The government agrees to hold a referendum in the south for self-determination in the year 2001.

1998 A new constitution drafted by the presidential committee goes into effect.

1999 Sudan hopes for peace during talks with Egypt. Africa's longest running civil war has left over 2 million dead and 4 million displaced.

2000 Prime Minister Ismail proposes an agenda for the Saharan summit, a meeting of various African countries to promote African unity.

1

Introducing Sudan

Sudan is a vast country of variety and extremes. The name Bilad al-Sudan—"land of the black people"—was given by Arab geographers in the Middle Ages to the area which includes modern Sudan. It is the largest country in Africa, the ninth largest in the world, and over 10 times the size of Britain. Over 1,250 miles (2,000 kilometers) separate the desert frontier with Egypt in the north from the rain forests bordering Uganda in the south.

Yet, with a canoe and enough time and energy it would be possible to travel the whole distance along just part of one river—the Nile, the longest river in the world. The White Nile enters Sudan in a rush through a narrow gorge on the Ugandan border. In the north, dammed at Aswan, it forms Lake Nubia, the world's largest man-made lake. Sudan has common borders with as many as eight African countries—Egypt, Libya, Chad, the Central African Republic, Democratic Republic of the Congo (Zaire), Uganda, Kenya, and Ethiopia. In general its frontiers do not fol-

An aerial view of the Nile River, the world's longest river, which flows through the entire length of Sudan.

low natural boundaries and many tribes spill over either side of these man-made borders.

There are five different zones of climate and vegetation within Sudan. The desert region, which accounts for a quarter of the total area; the semi-desert, in which the capital, Khartoum, is situated; the low-rainfall savannah; the high-rainfall savannah; and the mountain vegetation regions. The northern deserts rarely see rain, while in some parts of the south, it pours down nearly every day.

In these nearly one million square miles (two and a half million square kilometers) is a population of 33 million, 80 percent of whom are farmers or herdsmen living in small rural communities. Only one quarter of all Sudanese live in towns with more than 4,500 people; another quarter are nomadic. There are over 50 different tribes in Sudan, speaking over 100 different languages. The one common spoken language is Arabic.

14

A view of the desert region. One quarter of the land surface of Sudan is desert with this kind of scenery.

There are only a handful of towns of any size in the provinces. Yet as many as 2,700,000 people live in Khartoum, Khartoum North, and Omdurman, which are together known as the Three Towns, and lie at the junction of the White and Blue Niles.

Over 70 percent of the population of Sudan is Muslim, living mainly in the north. In the south of the country the majority of the people still practice the African religions of their ancestors, while 5 percent are Christians. With such diversity it is difficult to avoid tensions and conflict. However, since independence in 1956, Sudan has worked hard—through education, the newspapers, radio, and television—to develop a feeling among its people of belonging to one nation. This is not easy in such a vast and varied country, where journeys between towns may take several days by heavy-duty lorry over bumpy desert tracks; and where, in other areas, it is possible to be cut off for weeks during the rainy

15

In the 1980s Sudan had many refugees (from inside the country and from across the borders) fleeing from famine or war. These people have come from neighboring Eritrea.

season. Then there is the Sudd, the largest swamp in the world, which makes river transportation difficult between north and south on the White Nile.

Sudan is one of the 25 poorest countries in the world. Over 25 percent of the country's foreign currency comes from the sale of a single crop—cotton. To make matters worse, the rains have been poor in parts of northern Sudan in recent years, causing drought and even famine. In the 1980s, the famine reached catastrophic proportions with nearly three million people in western Sudan needing food aid.

Despite all their problems, the Sudanese are a patient, dignified, and hospitable people. Sudan is often overlooked and overshadowed by more important neighbors, but both the people and the country are well worth getting to know.

16

2

Early History

In about 750 B.C. a king named Piankhy left Napata, his capital in northern Sudan, and invaded Egypt to found the 25th Egyptian dynasty. His successors ruled over Egypt for about 100 years before finally being forced to retreat back to Napata. Then, in about 590 B.C., the capital was moved further south to Meroe, a city situated in the triangle between the Atbara and Nile rivers. More fertile than Napata, Meroe became the crossroads of important caravan routes. It was also well-supplied with iron ore and timber, the raw materials essential for iron smelting. The city flourished for a further 900 years until it was destroyed by the Ethiopians in 350 A.D. Although influenced by Egypt, the Meroitic civilization had many uniquely Sudanese features. There is also evidence that it had contacts with Rome, Greece, Persia, and even India at this time. Most importantly, it is thought that the art of iron working spread in the first century B.C. from Meroe to many other parts of the African continent. It was certainly iron production which maintained Meroe's power and wealth.

The kings of Meroe were buried beneath small, sharply-pointed pyramids. None of the pyramids was more than 30 feet (10 meters) high, and each had a small temple attached to its east face. As well as the pyramids, the remains of temples and palaces of this agricultural, cattle-rearing society can still be visited today. The carvings on them show some distinct Meroitic features—rather plump ladies and exotic animals such as elephants and lions.

After the decline of the Meroitic civilization in the fourth century A.D., three Christian kingdoms arose in Nubia—the vast area between Aswan (in the south of Egypt) and Sennar which lies south of Khartoum. They were known as Nobatia, Makurra, and Alwa.

Christianity, perhaps brought from Egypt by monks of the Coptic Church, probably existed in this area before the first official Christian mission arrived from Constantinople (modern Istanbul) in 543 A.D. Archaeologists have discovered remains of Christian buildings constructed before that date which suggest this. However, it is known for certain that two rival missions, belonging to different sects, were sent to Nubia in the sixth century—one by the Byzantine Emperor Justinian, and the other by his wife, Theodora.

The missionaries arrived bearing gold, rich baptismal robes, and other precious gifts. They had some success in converting the king and court to their beliefs, although Christianity is unlikely to have spread to the population as a whole. It must always have been rather an alien religion, using a foreign language, either Greek or Coptic, in its ritual until the ninth century when the vernacular Nubian language began to be used in the churches and in religious texts.

From the beautiful paintings which remain as evidence of this period, it is noticeable that the local Nubian people are shown with brown faces while angels and biblical characters have white, foreign faces.

Fortunately, archaeologists were able to excavate Christian buildings of this period before the flood caused by the construction of the Aswan High Dam in 1964. The raising and reconstruction of the temples at Abu Simbel in Egypt is famous, but it is not widely known that only 12 miles (19 kilometers) to the south, in a cathedral at Faras in Sudan, a team of Polish archaeologists uncovered 160 paintings dating from between the 8th and the 12th centuries. Some of these paintings, now housed in the National Museum in Khartoum, were hidden three layers deep beneath work of a later period. Many of them are amazingly well-preserved and colorful, having been protected by high banks of sand which had blown into the cathedral from the hot, dry desert. Within a radius of 35 miles (60 kilometers) of Faras, 60 different churches were located, indicating what an important Christian center this once was.

In 641 A.D. the Arabs brought Islam to the Egyptian-Nubian frontier. The Muslims and Christians signed a treaty, promising to live peacefully with each other. When, finally, the Christian kingdoms died out in Nubia at the end of the 14th century, it was probably as the result of a gradual spread of Islam through intermarriage rather than through armed conflict.

The style of this building shows how the civilization at Meroe came under foreign influence.

The spreading of the Muslim religion was further encouraged by trade, and by holy men who traveled throughout the area preaching. As the Christian kingdoms declined, Muslim Arabs penetrated from the north and from the Red Sea coast. At the same time, a ruling group known as the Funj, and its followers, moved into the area. The two forces clashed in battle in 1504 and the victorious Funj became the political masters, ruling through local Arab sheikhs.

For some 300 years, the Funj dynasty, known as the Black Sultanate, ruled from their capital named Sennar. Their authority covered a vast area of Sudan—from the Ethiopian border to the third cataract of the Nile River. European travelers who visited the royal court spoke of a palace with richly carved doorways, of women dressed in silk and wearing silver bracelets and anklets, of tournaments and mock battles, and of sheikhs paying tribute to their rulers with presents of slaves, camels, and horses.

But who were the Funj? Because there are so few written records from these times, we can only guess at their origins. Did they come from Ethiopia? Were they members of the Shilluk tribe which lives further south, or were they from some other dominant southern tribe which migrated northward? It is known that during this period Muslim holy men, called *fakis* traveled throughout the land teaching the Koran (the sacred book of Muslims), and that the Funj rulers were early converts to Islam. Thus the Muslim religion with its accompanying *Shari'a*, or code of justice, quickly spread throughout the Sultanate.

Eventually, the power of the Funj dynasty declined so that, by 1820, it was easy for Muhammad Ali, the viceroy of Egypt, to send his son Ismail to invade Sudan without bloodshed. Because, at that time, Egypt was a province of the Ottoman or Turkish Empire, this is known as the Turco-Egyptian conquest of Sudan. The country was to be ruled from Cairo for the next 60 years.

Muhammad Ali's aim was to exploit Sudan for gold and for slaves, some of whom were to be recruited into his army. Ismail's treatment of the Sudanese was harsh. As a result, in 1822, his camp was set on fire by a Sudanese leader, Mek Nimr, whom he had insulted. Ismail died in the fire; and today Mek Nimr is regarded as a national hero.

It was under the Turks that Khartoum became the military and administrative capital of Sudan. In 1839, Captain Salim, a Turkish sailor, explored the upper reaches of the White Nile, navigating

Harvesting sugarcane.

upstream as far as present-day Juba. However, disease was rife and only a few small military and trading posts were established.

It was at this time that agriculture was improved—more land was irrigated, new varieties of fruit trees were introduced, sugarcane and indigo were developed; and, most importantly, more cotton was grown. In addition, the telegraph system was established; the first length of railway track was laid; and a new, improved system of administration was set up. The port of Suakin on the Red Sea flourished. Also, towards the end of the period, Muhammad Ali's successors made a genuine attempt to stamp out the slave trade.

Suakin was a small town which came under Turkish authority in 1516 when the Turks conquered Egypt. From the 16th century it developed to become a major port on the west coast of the Red Sea.

Great caravans of 1,000 camels or more carried goods such as ivory, gum arabic (resin from the acacia tree), gold, ostrich feathers, hides, and slaves from the Sudanese interior to the port for export. The same caravans regularly left Suakin carrying imported spices, cottons, and silks to the towns of Berber and Kassala, from where they were distributed throughout Sudan. Trade was mainly with India, Ethiopia, Arabia, and Yemen. Sudanese and West African pilgrims also passed through the port on their way to the Muslim holy city of Mecca in Arabia.

Suakin was a beautiful town; its houses, shops, and mosques were built of coral rock covered with whitewashed plaster. Situated on a small, flat, oval island in a lagoon, it must have seemed to float on the surface of the sea. The elegant three- and four-story buildings were designed to exclude the sun and the hot wind from the mainland and to catch the cooling sea breezes. They were inhabited by wealthy merchants of many different nationalities.

With the opening of the Suez Canal, in 1869, the Red Sea increased in importance. But at the beginning of the 20th century, it was decided that the port of Suakin was no longer suitable for modern steamships and trading conditions. Instead, in 1906, Port Sudan was constructed some 40 miles (65 kilometers) to the north. It remains today Sudan's only major port. From the 1920s onward, Suakin declined rapidly although, even up to 1950, 20,000 pilgrims passed through the port each year on their way to Mecca.

The town of Suakin has fallen into decay but, as this picture shows, it still has a hint of its former charm.

Suakin is now a ghost town of crumbling buildings inhabited only by numerous cats, but it still has a hint of its former charm.

The slave trade has a very long history. Stone carvings of African slaves are to be found on the walls of the monuments of ancient Egypt. In the 10th century, slaves from Nubia, in the north of Sudan, were highly prized as soldiers in the Egyptian army. Slavery was not outlawed by the Muslim religion, but Islam did insist upon the good treatment of slaves, and encouraged the granting of freedom.

A system of domestic slavery also existed within Sudan. With constant inter-tribal fighting, there was a ready supply of captives to meet the demand for domestic servants, workers on the land, bodyguards, and concubines. Muslims also regarded the non-Muslim inhabitants of parts of Sudan as a source of supply for slaves.

Many of the buildings in Suakin, like this one, were beautifully decorated when they were new.

In the 19th century, Muhammad Ali, the Egyptian viceroy, wanted Sudanese slaves for his army. At about the same time, European and Arab traders penetrated the Upper White Nile area in search of ivory. There they set up *zaribas*—fortified trading posts—where slaves were required as porters and concubines. Slaves were also used, along with cattle, as barter for ivory. Thus, the ivory and slave trades were closely interlinked. Traditional tribal structures were deeply affected as a result of slavery, and some of the weaker tribes were nearly wiped out.

However, serious attempts were made to stamp out the slave trade. In 1854 Muhammad Ali closed the public slave market in Khartoum and a force of river police was set up to try and intercept the traders' boats on their return downstream. Two Englishmen, Samuel Baker and Charles Gordon, were both

An early illustration of an Arab slave raid.

employed in an attempt to put an end to this trade in human lives. But it was only the stable conditions of Anglo-Egyptian rule in the early 20th century that made this possible. Even so, the trade continued well into this century.

There is no doubt that memories of the Arab-dominated slave trade have contributed to the mistrust between Muslim and non-Muslim Sudanese.

In Sudanese history the period 1881-1898 is referred to as the *Mahdiya* as it marks the rule of Muhammad Ahmed, the Mahdi ("promised one") and his successor, the Khalifa Abdullahi. According to the Muslim religion, the Mahdi was a person sent by God to purify Islam and lead it back to its original simple ideals.

It was in 1881 that Muhammad Ahmed, a holy man living on Aba Island in the White Nile, south of Khartoum, declared him-

26

self to be this long-awaited person, with a message not only for Sudan but for the whole Muslim world. Many Sudanese of different tribes rallied around the Mahdi, who became a national as well as a religious leader.

In 1882, the British occupied Egypt and became worried about this "troublemaker" on their southern border. The following year, declaring a *jihad* (holy war), the Mahdi's followers successfully defeated 10,000 Egyptian troops under a British commander, Hicks Pasha, at the Battle of Shaykan near El Obeid. After this the Mahdi's troops went from victory to victory.

Something decisive needed to be done. In 1884, General Charles Gordon was sent to Khartoum with the task of withdrawing the Egyptian army from Sudan. But he delayed too long, and found himself a prisoner in the town, surrounded by the

Muhammed Ahmed— the Mahdi—who became a national and religious leader in 19th-century Sudan.

Mahdi's troops. The siege lasted several months and resulted, in January 1885, in the fall of Khartoum and the death of Gordon just two days before the arrival of the relief expedition which had been sent from Britain. This marked the end of foreign rule and the beginning of Sudan's first religious state.

Only six months after Gordon's death, the Mahdi also died. He was succeeded by the Khalifa Abdullahi. There followed a difficult time for Sudan, with years of famine and a smallpox epidemic.

Although British public opinion was outraged at what it regarded as Gordon's unnecessary death, it was not until 1896 that Britain again became actively involved in Sudan. In that year, an Anglo-Egyptian army, under the command of Herbert Kitchener, was sent south from Egypt. As it advanced, it constructed a railway at the incredible rate—for such difficult desert conditions—of one and a half miles (two and a half kilometers) per day. Kitchener was then able to bring up supplies as the railway advanced.

On September 2, 1898, Kitchener's army of 24,000 men met over 50,000 of the Khalifa's troops at the Battle of Omdurman, some six miles (nine kilometers) to the north of that town, on a plain near the Kerari Hills. Six hours of fighting resulted in a decisive victory for the Anglo-Egyptian side. In spite of the great personal courage of the Sudanese troops, it was the victory of a modern army equipped with the latest weapons (such as the Maxim and Gatling guns) against an army armed for the most part only with swords, spears, and religious conviction. A young man named Winston Churchill, who was later to become the British prime minister, took part in the battle, and wrote an

Gordon Memorial College. Its buildings are now part of the University of Khartoum.

account of it entitled *The River War*. After the victory, Kitchener set about reconstructing the town of Khartoum. The era of joint Anglo-Egyptian rule over Sudan, known as the Condominium, then began.

The general public in Britain believed that Kitchener's action was revenge for Gordon's death some 13 years earlier. However, in politics all is not always as it seems. The scramble for Africa was on! The British government was anxious to gain a foothold in this part of Africa since the Italians were already established in Ethiopia to the east and the Belgians in the Congo to the south-west. So, after the Battle of Omdurman, Kitchener received instructions to make his way as quickly as possible to a place called Fashoda, further south on the White Nile. There he confronted a French expedition under Captain Marchand. Traveling on foot and by boat, these brave French soldiers had made an incredible, two-year journey, along the Congo River and its tributaries, from the west coast of Africa to the banks of the Nile, where Captain Marchand claimed the area for France. After heated negotiations between London and Paris, which nearly led to war, the French finally withdrew, leaving the Anglo-Egyptian Condominium in control of Sudan until independence in 1956.

3

From Condominium to Independence

After the Battle of Omdurman, the Khalifa and some of his surviving commanders fled to Kordofan, in the west. The Khalifa was later killed there in another battle and, not long afterward, the whole of the northern part of the country was brought under control.

There was, however, one exception. This was Ali Dinar, the independent Sultan of Darfur. He held on to his sultanate, in the far west of Sudan, until 1916.

Kitchener himself became the first governor general of Anglo-Egyptian Sudan, or the Condominium ("joint rule"). During the next 20 years the pattern of regions (each headed by a governor), provinces, and districts was established. It has survived with little change to this day.

For the British government the aim of the Omdurman campaign was to stop the advance into Africa of other rival powers, such as the French, Belgians, and Italians. For the British man in the street it was also to avenge the death of General Gordon. On the other hand, the British claimed to the Egyptians, who had ruled Sudan before the rise of the Mahdi, that their aim was to recover Sudan for the Khedive (Viceroy) in Cairo.

However, once the British had gained power, they did not want to establish a true partnership, a real "joint rule," with Egypt. This was partly out of self-interest but also because, in Britain, some people saw Mahdism as a popular uprising against Egyptian rule. This, indeed, is the way the Sudanese today remember the Mahdiya. So, while the flags of the two nations flew side by side, the British governors-general—and all of them were British—held the real power. Egypt, meanwhile, had to bear the cost of having its troops based in Sudan and had to make grants and interest-free loans for the development of the country.

As the years went by, Egypt's role in Sudan became even smaller. Following violent disturbances in Cairo in 1919 and the murder of the governor general of Sudan, Sir Lee Stack, in 1924, all Egyptian soldiers serving in Sudan were expelled.

Sudan, like many nations in Africa today, did not exist as a separate state until independence. Its borders were decided by agreements made with neighboring colonial powers. So, for example, the British and French agreed that the watershed between the Nile and Congo rivers should be the boundary in the southwest of the country. This left some tribes, such as the Azande, straddling both sides of the frontier. Indeed, nearly all Sudan's land borders divide people who share the same culture and language.

In the early years of the Condominium, the railway system was

Harvesting cotton, Sudan's most important export today.

rapidly developed in the north to improve communications between Khartoum (once again the capital) and the provincial towns, and between Khartoum and the Red Sea coast, where Port Sudan was expanding. In 1926, the Gezira Scheme was opened. This was to become the world's largest cooperative farming project for the production of cotton—Sudan's most important export.

From 1922, the government put into practice the policy of indirect rule. Tribal leaders and chiefs were made responsible for most local government, including justice and tax collection. This strengthened traditional tribal authority and limited the political power of the educated Sudanese in the towns who were beginning to resent British rule. It also restricted the influence of rising leaders such as Abd al-Rahman al-Mahdi, son of the Mahdi.

Under Turco-Egyptian rule, control over much of the south was limited to the setting up of a number of trading and military posts.

33

During the Mahdiya this control became even looser. So British administrators in the south particularly welcomed indirect rule since it allowed them to govern while disturbing traditional societies as little as possible.

However, the British went much further than this and decided to limit the influence of the north in the three southern regions. Many southerners were afraid of being dominated by the more developed north. So, in 1922, the southern regions became "closed districts." Many northern merchants and traders, known as *jellaba,* were made to leave the south; and southerners who wanted to go north in search of work were discouraged. The British also tried to limit the spread of both Islam and the Arabic

A Shilluk king. In the past, tribal leaders had considerable influence in Sudan.

language in the south. At the same time, Christian missionaries were allowed to convert the people from their African religions and to set up schools where the lessons were taught in English.

Just before the Second World War began, a group was formed which seriously opposed Condominium rule for the first time. This was the Graduates' Congress. It represented all Sudanese who had received education beyond primary level. Its members were young and impatient because there was not even a long-term plan for the country to become independent. Its first general secretary was Ismail al-Azhari, later to become the first prime minister of independent Sudan.

Two main political parties gradually emerged—the Ashigga ("Blood Brothers") Party, which later became the National Unionist Party, and the Umma ("Nation") Party. Both had an appeal beyond tribal loyalty and remained influential until political parties were banned after the 1989 military coup.

One important difference between the two parties was the way they visualized Sudan and Egypt once independence had been achieved. The Unionists, as their name suggests, wanted to join with their northern neighbor and spoke of "the unity of the Nile Valley." The Umma Party, on the other hand, argued for a completely independent Sudan—"Sudan for the Sudanese."

In 1952, King Farouk of Egypt was overthrown. General Neguib, who had strong connections with Sudan, came to power. In early 1953, a new Anglo-Egyptian agreement was signed. The two countries agreed to a period of up to three years to prepare

The mosque in Khartoum built by King Farouk of Egypt during the period of Anglo-Egyptian rule in Sudan.

Sudan for full independence and to allow an elected Constituent Assembly to draw up a constitution for the new state.

The last British and Egyptian troops withdrew from Sudan in November 1955. On January 1, 1956, both the British and Egyptian flags were lowered in the grounds of the palace on the banks of the Blue Nile, and the flag of the independent, sovereign state of Sudan was raised. Sudan was to retain close and friendly ties with both partners in the Condominium which had controlled it for nearly 60 years.

4

Islam, Christianity, and Other Religions

Within 30 years of the death of the Prophet Muhammad, in 632 A.D., the Arabs had burst out of Arabia, and Islam had swept from Morocco in the west to present-day Pakistan in the east. Even though Islam spread through Sudan much later, Sudanese Muslims feel a strong tie with their Muslim brothers, both Arab and non-Arab.

The Prophet Muhammad was born in about 570 A.D. in the town of Mecca, an important religious and commercial center. When he was 40 years old, he was visited one night as he sat in prayer, by the Angel Jibril (Gabriel) who told him that he had been chosen as a messenger or prophet of Allah. (Allah is the Arabic word for God.)

Muhammad gathered around him, in the town of Mecca, a band of devoted followers who believed in Islam, the new religion. But in 622 A.D. his enemies plotted to kill him and his followers. Muhammad, hearing of their plans, fled to the town of

Yathrib, later to be known to all Muslims as Medina, "the city." The Muslim calendar, which is a lunar one (based upon the movements of the moon), begins from the date of their flight, the *Hejira*. So, for example, the year 1985 A.D. corresponds to 1405 A.H. in the Muslim calendar.

The sacred book of the Muslims, the Koran, is made up of God's revelations to Muhammad, through the Angel Gabriel. These revelations were memorized by his closest followers and written down. The Koran, Muslims believe, is literally the word of God. Not one word has been changed since it was first written down; nor, having been revealed in Arabic, can it be adequately translated.

Islamic law, known as *Shari'a*, comprises the rules which govern people's behavior. It is based upon the Koran and the *Sunna*, a summary of the behavior and sayings of Muhammad. In many Muslim countries, the legal system is a mixture of Islamic and European law. This was so in Sudan until 1983, when the then President Nimeiri introduced his very harsh interpretation of *Shari'a* law, which in the view of many sincere Sudanese Muslims was against the true spirit of Islam.

A Muslim has much in common with both Christians and Jews. His religion recognizes only one God and six major prophets: Adam, Nuh (Noah), Ibrahim (Abraham), Musa (Moses), Isa Jesus), and of course Muhammad himself—according to Muslims, the last and greatest of the line. Like Christians, Muslims believe in a time at the end of the world when all people will be judged. According to Islam, everyone will be made to walk over the

The Two Niles Mosque, opened in 1984. It is situated at the junction of the Blue and White Niles in Khartoum.

bridge between heaven and hell, which will be finer than a hair and sharper than a sword, and from which the wicked will plunge.

There are five main duties which a Muslim is bound to perform, unless he is prevented by sickness or poverty. These duties are known as the five pillars of the faith. First, he must be ready to declare that there is only one God and that Muhammad is his prophet or messenger. Second, he must say his prayers regularly. A strict Muslim prays five times a day. Many sincere Muslims pray less often than this but few will omit to pray at sunset. Preparations for prayer, the form of prayer, and the gestures which accompany it are all laid down in great detail. Before praying, a Muslim must purify himself by washing in a prescribed order—hands, mouth, nostrils, face, forearms, hands, and feet. In

39

mosques there is often a pool for this purpose. Islam is, however, a very individual, personal religion; at sunset a merchant will pray outside his shop; or a bus will stop, and the driver and passengers will pray by the roadside. It is a great honor to be chosen by a group of friends or colleagues to step forward and lead them in prayer. The only essential is to face toward the holy city of Mecca while bowing, kneeling, and touching the forehead to the ground, all in a set sequence.

The third duty required of a Muslim is the giving of alms to the poor, normally in the proportion of one-fortieth of his wealth.

A Muslim, except if he is sick or traveling, should also fast from daybreak until sunset during the holy month of Ramadan. As the Muslim calendar is a lunar one, Ramadan moves forward by 10 days each year. Great self-discipline is needed for Muslims to deny themselves even a drop of water during the hot season in Sudan when the midday temperature is regularly above 104 degrees Fahrenheit (40 degrees Celsius) and daylight lasts for over 12 hours. Children usually start fasting from about the age of 12.

Last, a Muslim who is able to do so should perform the *hajj* (pilgrimage) to the holy city of Mecca at least once in his lifetime. In former days, Sudanese pilgrims, together with many who had traveled from further west, used to sail across the Red Sea from the port of Suakin to Jeddah in Arabia, where they joined millions of other Muslims from all over the world. Nowadays, however, nearly all pilgrims travel by air. At the time of departure, Khartoum airport is packed with pilgrims, bareheaded and wearing only two pieces of white unseamed cloth as a sign of humility.

40

Muslims are required to wash before praying. This man has reached the last in the prescribed order of parts of the body to be washed—his feet— before he says his prayers.

The mosque is the most important meeting place in the Muslim village or community. It is simple in design, but in Sudan it is often painted in bright colors. The only special features inside are the *mihrab*, a niche which indicates the direction of Mecca; and a *minbar* (pulpit), from which the sermon will be delivered at Friday prayers—Friday being the Muslim day of rest. The call to prayer resounds from the slender tower of the minaret. Traditionally, the muezzin who calls people to prayer, climbed the steps of the minaret five times a day. Nowadays, however, loudspeakers are generally used.

For the Sudanese Muslim, Islam is very much a part of his everyday life. His conversation is peppered with greetings and

Khartoum airport—the departure point for many pilgrims on their way to Mecca. In the past they sailed across the Red Sea.

expressions referring to Allah. In English, the original meaning of "goodbye" is "God be with thee." For the Muslim the literal meaning is still very much in his mind. When friends leave he will say "*maa assalama*," "go in safety," to which they reply "*Allah yisalli-mak*," "may Allah give you safety." Even more commonly, when planning anything in the future such as a journey or a meeting, he will always begin with "*insha Allah*," "if God wills." Similarly, if something pleasant happens, he must never forget to say "*alham-du lillah*," "may God be praised."

The basic beliefs and practices of Islam are common to the whole of the Muslim world. However, in Sudan there are one or two special features. For example, the Mahdi is regarded by the Sudanese today mainly as a nationalist leader, the "Father of

42

Independence." In his time, however, his followers in Sudan believed him to be the expected leader whose arrival heralded the end of the world.

Islam was taken to many remote parts of Sudan by traveling merchants who, although they knew all about the five pillars and the basic practices of Islam, were not much concerned with theory.

In contrast, there are *fakis* and *sheikhs* (holy men) who devote their lives to the study and teaching of Islam. The most famous of these have groups of followers, organized in *tarigas* or religious orders. The tombs of these holy men are usually in the form of a cone-shaped building, called a *gubba*. Villagers visit such shrines to ask the faki or sheikh to help in the answering of their prayers, even though, according to strict Islamic belief, there are no saints to act as go-between between man and God.

Sometimes, especially during popular festivals such as the Prophet Muhammad's birthday, groups of men can be seen swaying and chanting together, repeating over and over the name of Allah or phrases from the Koran. This is the *zikr* ceremony where, as the drums beat and the atmosphere becomes more charged, the men enter into a hypnotic trance, which they believe brings them closer to God. Every Friday, in the desert outside Omdurman, men in spotless white robes called *jallabiyas* and white turbans called *emmas*, meet with others (dressed in the patched green robes of holy men) in front of the tomb of Sheikh Hamed al-Nil. He was a faki whose body, according to legend, was washed up on shore in perfect condition over two months after he was drowned.

43

Those in the center of the big circle stamp, sway, and chant to the rhythm of the drums, while individuals break away to whirl quickly. All aim to bring themselves closer to God.

For Muslims, there are two major religious holidays (*Eids*). The *Eid al-Fitr*, the Feast of the Breaking of the Fast, also known as the Small Eid, marks the end of Ramadan. Just as at Christmas time in other countries, at this time children in Sudan receive presents, often of new clothes, and families go from house to house, visiting friends and relatives.

The *Eid al-Adha*, the Feast of the Sacrifice, or Great Eid, is also a time of present giving and general happiness. All families who can afford it slaughter a sheep and give part of the meat to the

A *gubba*—the tomb of a holy man.

Men taking part in the *zikr* ceremony.

poor, remembering how Abraham was ready to sacrifice his son Isaac.

Children also look forward to the Prophet Muhammad's birthday, the time when pink sugar dolls and sticky sweets with nuts and sesame seeds are sold from special booths, and when street entertainers—conjurors, acrobats, and sometimes even trained monkeys, perform in the town squares.

Approximately 5 percent of the population of Sudan is Christian. In the north, in the capital and main towns, there are Christians whose ancestors came to settle in Sudan from Egypt, Syria, Lebanon, and Greece during the last 170 years.

In the south, however, Christianity plays a much more important role. During the Condominium, the government allocated separate areas to Catholic and Protestant missionaries in which they established schools, churches, and clinics. Most people in southern Sudan still follow the African religions of their tribes. However, many of the educated southerners—government officials, army officers, teachers, and so on—were converted to Christianity as they received their education in mission schools. Although quite few in number, these people have a great influence in southern society.

Twenty-five percent of the population of Sudan still follow ancient tribal beliefs. Many of these African religions are based upon a remote god, and a respect for tribal ancestors who are believed to be closely involved in people's daily lives. Indeed, it is thought that the ancestors, if neglected or annoyed, send sickness, misfortune, or death. People also believe in spirits which inhabit natural objects, such as stones, rivers, and trees. Any event which is slightly out of the ordinary may be seen to have a religious significance, often requiring a sacrifice to be made. Different clans in a tribe will often have their own totem—a plant or animal with which they are particularly associated and which is regarded as the ancestor of the clan. Members of the clan respect their particular totem, and no one would harm it, even if it is a dangerous animal such as a crocodile.

The Shilluk people, for example, worship Juok whom they believe to be the supreme god who created mankind.

Another god, known as Nyikang, is seen as the founder of their

46

A village church in the Nuba mountains, in southern Sudan where Christianity plays an important role.

nation, possessing all the ideal Shilluk qualities. Shilluk folk stories tell how Nyikang defeated the original inhabitants of the land, whose leader was the sun. Nyikang then revived his army by sprinkling his warriors with water. Today, Nyikang is called the "Bringer of Rain" and is still believed to revive his people by calling down the rains after the dry season.

Shilluk kings are considered divine because they embody the spirit of Nyikang. When a king dies, the declaration made is: "There is no land. Shilluk country ceases to be." A new king must then be chosen from among princes who are supported by rival groups.

The Shilluk revere their ancestors and believe in spirits which live in the bush and river. The most important of these—for this

A Shilluk fishing festival. This tribe are famed for their skill as fishermen. Their religion includes belief in spirits who live in the rivers.

tribe famed for their skill as fishermen—are the river people who are believed to own ghost herds of cattle which live in the river.

For the Shilluk, the two most important religious occasions in each year are the rainmaking ceremony, and the harvest festival which takes place after the millet has been cut. Both are important to a community which lives from the land.

5

The People of Sudan

Sudan is a vast country with over 50 separate tribal groups, and over 100 different languages. Add to this a climate which varies widely from area to area, and the enormous difference between life in the town and life in the country, and it is easy to understand the wide range of people covered by the name Sudanese.

Some of them are herdsmen, some are farmers; some are nomadic, others are settled. In the north, most of them speak Arabic as their mother tongue; in the south, many different languages are spoken among the tribes.

The largest group in the south is the Dinka. Like many other peoples in this area, their lives revolve around their cattle which serve as a form of currency and prestige as well as providing for many of their needs. The cattle dung is burned as fuel, while the ash from the dung fire is smeared on the body to keep mosquitoes at bay. The urine may be used for washing, or to dye the hair. The milk is drunk and the skin serves as a mattress. Nothing is

These people are Rashaida nomads. They belong to a Sudanese tribe which came from Saudi Arabia about 100 years ago.

wasted. Dinka ox-songs, composed in honor of their cattle, are famous. Here is an example:

My Mijok is important to me
Like tobacco and the pipe;
When there is no tobacco
The pipe goes out.
His pace and mine are the same.

When a boy comes of age he is given an ox and takes a name relating to a description of the animal, which then becomes a kind of soulmate for him.

Traditionally, Sudan is seen as the point where northern Arab

50

A Dinka cattle camp. There are some three million Dinka people in southern Sudan, where they form the largest group.

meets black African and the two blend together. In general, this is true, but in such a process there are bound to be conflicts. There has been civil war between the north and the south since the 1950s and there has been some tension over the exploitation of oil and the digging of the Jonglei Canal in the south which had to be halted due to conflicts there. In addition, travel is difficult, even impossible, in some areas during the rainy season. The long-term aim—and it will be difficult to achieve—is national unity which, at the same time, recognizes people's right to their differences.

Housing offers a good example of some of the regional and tribal differences. In the extreme north, where it is very hot and dry, the Nubians build thick-walled, flat-topped mud houses with highly ornamented doorways. The average small-town dweller throughout the country lives in a baked-brick, one-story house arranged around one or more courtyards to allow women to lead their own lives for the most part separately from the men. In rural areas, especially in the south where there is more rain, people live in *ghotiya*—circular straw huts with pointed roofs made from millet stalks, sometimes with a straw fence round them to create a compound.

Among the nomads, the style of tent differs according to the tribe. For example, in the eastern region, the Rashaida weave their distinctive striped tents out of goat hair. However, they live alongside the Hadendowa, who construct their tents out of palm-fiber mats.

Sudan could be called a very young country. Forty-five percent of the population is under the age of 15; and 97 percent is under the age of 64. Life expectancy at birth is about 55 years. Children are much wanted and families are large. It is quite usual for people to have five children and not uncommon to find families with as many as 10. The extended family is very important—distant aunts, uncles, and cousins may be as close as brothers and sisters in other societies.

There are certain family duties which everyone in Sudan observes—hospitality, financial help, and attendance at all the important landmarks in life, such as births, weddings, and funerals. In addition, much entertainment is family-based.

Weddings are a colorful and important part of Sudanese social life. The extended family and friends of both the bride and groom

A *ghotiya*—circular straw hut with a pointed roof made of millet stalks.
This type of home is typical of rural areas in southern Sudan.

will be invited; so, for a middle-class wedding, hundreds of people will join together for festivities lasting several days. Most Sudanese marriages are arranged by the parents, often between cousins, second cousins, or other members of the family. If their children marry outside the family, the parents will usually try to choose someone belonging to the same tribe and certainly to the same social class.

Middle-class parents in the towns start looking around for a husband for their daughter once she has finished secondary school education and is about 19 or 20 years old. In country areas, girls tend to get married earlier. A man is ready to marry when he has enough money to provide his bride with the standard of living she was used to at home. This often means that he will be some years older than his bride.

53

Once the parents have a possible bride or groom in mind, discreet investigations will begin. Will she be a capable housewife? Is he mean? Has he got a good reputation? All these and many other questions will be asked. Only after the parents are satisfied with the answers will the other family be approached, perhaps with a photograph. Then negotiations will begin in order to settle what clothes, gold jewelry, and furniture the bridegroom must provide.

Even today it is possible for a Sudanese bride and groom never to have seen or talked to one another before they are married. This is because physical appearance is considered to be of less importance than other qualities. The marriage is seen as being between two families as much as between two individuals, and both bride and groom have a clear idea of the traditional roles of husband and wife.

Although both men and women guests will be invited to a wedding, they are usually entertained in separate parts of the house and garden. The first day of celebrations takes place in the groom's house. It is called the henna night, when the groom's hands and feet are dyed a dark brown using henna paste. The bride will not be present but all the groom's family and friends will be there. The next day, attention moves to the bride's house and, from early morning, there is great activity and singing. The bride has all her body hair removed with a mixture of sugar and water boiled up to a sticky paste, and her hands are decorated with patterns painted in henna. Then she takes a smoke bath, squatting for hours over a pit full of special smouldering wood so

A merchant outside a gold shop in the bazaar. Gold is a significant feature of marriage arrangements, as part of the bride's dowry.

that the perfumed smoke will scent her whole body and give her skin a golden sheen. As a married woman she will repeat this beauty treatment regularly.

The religious part of the marriage ceremony is simply the signing of a contract in the presence of a *faki*, who recites some verses of the Koran. The bride and groom do not usually attend this ceremony but are represented by their male relatives.

Another party for hundreds of guests begins early on the second evening. Enormous quantities of food and soft drinks are served. If there is not enough room for the guests in the house and garden, then a brightly colored awning will be put up in the street outside, perhaps even blocking it completely. No one minds the inconvenience and noise; all the neighbors have been invited anyway!

55

The bride may wear a western-style, white wedding dress or a more traditional short, red one. The bridal pair sit on a raised platform to receive the congratulations of the guests. The bride should hold her eyes modestly down and not look too cheerful or eager at the idea of being married. Later that night, covered in gold jewelry, the bride performs the "pigeon dance," in front of the groom and female guests. She will have been practicing for months in advance and dances with her chest thrust out, and her head moving backwards and forwards like a pigeon. Other girls may also dance at the party. This is when young men may try to catch a glimpse of a possible future bride!

On the third morning there may be further dancing, and the hands of the bride and groom are joined with silk thread. Some time later that day the couple may slip away on honeymoon. The newlyweds often live in the girl's parents' house until the birth of their first child, which everyone hopes will take place within the first year of marriage.

For Muslims, other celebrations center around religious occasions, such as the return home of a pilgrim from the holy city of Mecca, the circumcision of a child, the Prophet Muhammad's birthday, or the two major religious holidays—the *Eids*. At all these happy events the women can be heard giving high-pitched cries of joy, called *zagareet*. Friday is the day of rest for Muslims, like Sunday for Christians. The weekly holiday, therefore, differs in the south and north of Sudan. For men in Sudan the club is the main place of entertainment. Even the smallest village often has a farmers' or merchants' club where the men go to chat or play cards.

Sudanese children are rarely seen playing in the street with toys, though they often show great inventiveness in making small cars out of odds and ends of metal, and in constructing elaborate miniature villages from mud.

Soccer is a very popular activity for boys and young men. Every village has its soccer pitch; and most evenings, as the sun sets, there is a game in progress. In towns, the cinema and television are popular. And almost everyone, even in the most remote villages, has access to a transistor radio.

The *zar* is a ceremony for women. The aim of the *zar* is to cure a woman by soothing the spirits which possess her. In addition, it provides a good deal of entertainment. A group of women, the leaders of the *zar*, will beat out a rhythm with drums and rattles. If the woman's spirit is moved, she will get to her feet and dance to the rhythm, often using objects associated with her particular

A Sudanese bride, wearing heavy gold jewelry.

spirit—a cigarette, an item of red clothing, a stick. *Zar* ceremonies may last up to seven days. They sometimes provide a woman with more freedom than her life normally allows.

Many Sudanese men wear western dress. Because of the heat, this is usually just trousers and a shirt without a tie, even on formal occasions. However, the white *jallabiya* (robe) with a white *emma* (turban) has long been traditional wear in the north. This is what men wear when relaxing at home and also what they wear on special occasions. The women dress in western-style clothes. In the north, they then wrap around themselves about 10 yards (nine meters) of fine, semi-transparent cloth called a *tobe*. The *tobe* conceals the outlines of the body but leaves the face exposed. Very often it is chosen to blend in color with the clothes worn underneath, which can occasionally be glimpsed. Office wear is usually a white *tobe*. In the privacy of her own home, a woman will remove her *tobe*. In some parts of Sudan there are still tribes who feel most comfortable when they are naked, even in public, though there is increasing pressure against this.

Some Sudanese, both men and women, have facial scars. From evidence on Meroitic friezes, it is known that scarring is a very ancient custom. The scars show that someone belongs to a certain tribe. They are also proof of great courage. Shilluk, for example, bear a row of raised bumps across the base of the forehead. Another tribe, the Nuer, have a series of six parallel lines on the forehead, while the Ja'aliin tribe have lines marked on the cheek.

58

Among women, scarring is often thought to be a mark of beauty. Many northern village women also have their bottom lip tattooed, giving it a strange blue color. Among the southern tribes, a woman may have her whole body crisscrossed with scars. These immediately indicate whether she is married or not, whether she has had her first child, and so on. Although still seen quite frequently among the older generation, scarring is a custom which is gradually dying out.

Visitors are generally surprised at the small size of the shops and the lack of choice of things to buy in Sudan. Even in the capital, Khartoum, there is nothing resembling a supermarket or department store. Usually the husband takes care of most of the day-to-day shopping. After the age of 40, however, women are considered old enough to be given more freedom of movement! In the country areas, women have always been more free, since they are needed to help with the work outside the home. In the towns, a greater number of women are now working, as life becomes increasingly expensive and more and more families need a second income.

Most food is fresh and therefore seasonal. There are often shortages of basic food products, such as sugar, bread, and eggs. In addition, on two days of the week, meat is not on sale. To preserve food, the Sudanese often dry it. One example is meat, which they cut into strips and hang up in the sun. They then pound it into a powder and add fresh or dried vegetables to it to make a stew.

Most people cook on charcoal which burns in a simple tin barbecue called a *kanoon*. Cooking often takes place in the open air, in the courtyard or compound, perhaps under a lean-to to provide shade. Indeed, many activities which normally happen indoors in more temperate climates take place outside in Sudan because of the heat. For most of the year in the north, it is cooler to sleep in the open air. During the day, visitors are entertained in the courtyard, and the string beds are used as sofas.

The greatest way to honor a guest in Sudan is to slaughter a sheep for him. The animal is killed and then cut up. A great delicacy is *marara*–a mixture of the sheep's raw intestines, along with the liver and the lungs, carefully washed and eaten with a lot of chilli pepper. For most people, however, meat is a luxury. The Sudanese eat a lot of vegetables in stews and salads. The staple grain is millet, made either into *asida* (a kind of porridge) or into a flat, pancake-type bread called *kisra*.

People usually eat from a common bowl, using their right hand. The Sudanese are very hospitable and a passerby will always be invited to sit down and join in the meal. In the same way, visits to offices or friends involve a non-stop stream of tea, coffee, and sodas. Although Sudanese do not eat many sweets or desserts they always take three or four teaspoons of sugar in their hot drinks.

The working day for offices is from 8:00 A.M. to 2:00 P.M. Shops are usually open during these hours, too, and they reopen at about 6:00 P.M. for another three hours. Before people go to work, they normally have only a cup of tea. Then, around 9:30

Most cooking in Sudan is done in the open air.

A.M., everything stops for the real breakfast of beans, salad, liver, and bread, or a fish sandwich.

Some of the most common illnesses in Sudan are stomach upsets, hepatitis, malaria, and bilharzia. Bilharzia, a disease which saps energy and affects the liver, is contracted through water-borne larvae which penetrate the skin. The waters of the White Nile contain bilharzia larvae; but, so far, the Blue Nile is said to be uninfected. The increase in irrigation and in the density of population has spread bilharzia even more widely. Throughout Africa, 60 million people are said to suffer from this serious disease. However, once it is identified, it can be quite easily cured.

Folk customs in Sudan are often a blend of many different beliefs. For example, when a baby is born it is quite possible that the family will whisper the name of Allah in his ear (a Muslim custom), make the sign of the cross in water on his forehead (a Christian custom), and protect him with an amulet or lucky charm consisting of the bone from a Nile fish (a custom pre-dating both Christianity and Islam).

Like other peoples in Africa and the Middle East, many Sudanese believe in the power of the "evil eye." This means that someone may take away another person's good fortune by envy. The symbol of a hand or an eye with an arrow through it is said to break the power of the evil eye. Many people wear an amulet or lucky charm around the neck or arm to protect them from its power.

6

The Farmer and the Herdsman

Sudan is an agricultural country with 80 percent of its population living from the land. Most people are subsistence farmers, growing only enough for their own needs, with little extra to spare. Yet agricultural products make up 90 percent of the country's exports and 35 percent of government revenue. Even so, Sudan could be much more productive than it is. It has been estimated that only 10 percent of possible arable land is at present being used. Much more could be cultivated if only channels could be dug for irrigation, and fuel could be guaranteed for water pumps. In the 1970s there were high hopes that Sudan would become "the breadbasket of the Arab world." However, far from a food surplus, there has been severe drought and even famine in some areas, as the desert has advanced and the rainfall decreased in recent years. In 1985, for example many of the people of Darfur and Kordofan in western Sudan had to abandon their villages and seek refuge in camps outside the towns in the hope of finding food there.

Subsistence farmers.

The first large-scale agricultural project was the Gezira Scheme, set up by the British after the First World War to produce cotton. *Gezira* is the Arabic word for island. It refers to the area of land south of Khartoum between the arms of the Blue and the White Niles. The Blue Nile was dammed at Sennar and a network of irrigation canals was dug which served a 250,000 acres (101,175 hectares) of land.

Today, over 2,000,000 acres (800,000 hectares) are under cultivation and some 200,000 farmers are members of the scheme and have contracts with the Gezira Board. The farmers provide the labor for growing cotton and other crops for their own use or for sale. The Board, which owns the land, sprays the crops, sells the cotton, and maintains the vital irrigation canals and machinery. Profits are then divided equally.

64

Cotton is still Sudan's main export, providing 30 percent of the country's badly needed foreign earnings. Because world prices for cotton slumped while production costs rose, Sudan has tried to grow a greater variety of different crops and not to depend so much on cotton. Other major crops are *dura, dukhn,* and *sorghum*—which are all types of millet—groundnuts, sesame seed, maize, wheat, and castor. The fruits which are grown are dates, mangoes, guavas, citrus fruits, and bananas.

Sudan is also the world's largest exporter of gum arabic. This is the resin of certain types of acacia tree. It is usually collected in Kordofan in the west by large numbers of people. Once exported, it is used in medicines, glues, and sweets. Fruit gums, for example, will almost certainly have started off life as the resin of a tree growing in the semi-desert region of Sudan.

There are many problems facing agriculture in Sudan. Desertification is a major one: the desert in the west is creeping forward at the rate of almost two miles (three kilometers) every year. This is because often too many trees are chopped down for fuel or charcoal, or because goats and sheep strip bushes which then die so that their roots no longer retain the topsoil. The watertable (the level below which the soil or rock is saturated with water) is also falling, with the result that it is necessary to dig deeper and deeper to find water.

The Blue and White Niles flood each year and they bring with them fertile silt which makes the land more productive. The Blue Nile, which flows from Ethiopia, bears the most silt as it is a faster-flowing river than the White Nile, which has its source in

One of the major problems in Sudan is that much of the land is turning to desert like this.

Uganda, and tends to be broader and shallower. The flood of the White Nile begins in April in southern Sudan, but it is not until August and September that the 20-foot (six-meter) rise in water is obvious in Khartoum. At that time, the area upstream from the town looks more like a broad lake than a river.

A number of important but small-scale dams have been constructed to regulate the flow of the Niles and to provide hydroelectric power. It was the Sennar Dam, opened on the Blue Nile in 1925, which first made year-round cultivation possible. Then came the Jebel Awliya Dam on the White Nile above Khartoum and, more recently, the Khashm al-Girba Dam on the Atbara River, and the Roseires Dam on the Blue Nile near the Ethiopian border.

Because Egypt also depends on the Nile waters which first flow through Sudan, there are agreements between the two countries as to how much water each may use every year.

As a result of years of drought in Ethiopia and low levels of rain in southern Sudan, in 1985 the Nile was at its lowest level for 80 years. Drought has continued to plague the area through the 1990s. This has meant times of hardship and famine for Sudan (as throughout its history) until the rains again fall in plenty, inside and outside its borders.

The old methods of irrigation in Sudan are the *sagia* (water-wheel) and the *shaduf* (water-sweep) which raises water using a counterweight. These have now been largely replaced by small mechanical diesel pumps. The steady thumping noise which the pumps make is a familiar sound along the rivers and canals. Once

Constructing a Sudanese dam. Dams have been constructed to regulate the flow of the Nile and produce hydroelectric power.

Children fetching water from the canal.

the water has been raised to the required level it is then directed to the crops through an intricate network of channels which the farmer blocks and unblocks to ensure that all parts of his land are watered.

However, not all areas of Sudan need irrigation. To the south, out of the desert and semi-desert zones, there are areas where rain-fed agriculture is possible. In this varied country, rainfall ranges from near-zero in the north to 47 inches (120 centimeters) per year in the extreme south which has a rainy season lasting from eight to nine months.

The Sudanese have always been aware of the need to store water in times of plenty in order to use it at dry times of the year. Some of their methods of water storage are ingenious. In the west, for example, the trunk of the baobab tree is often hollowed out, given a coating of pitch, and filled with water so that it acts as a kind of well. *Hafirs* (reservoirs) are another method. To make a reservoir, a *khor* (a river which flows only during the brief rainy season) is dammed, and then the ground is hollowed out to retain the water. Finally, the area is fenced, to keep animals away.

Wells are vital for the survival of the remote villages. The government has therefore sunk many borewells to ensure a constant supply of water. Even so, women and children often have to walk long distances each day to fetch enough water for their needs. There are also donkey-drawn watercarts which travel from village to village selling water.

Not every family in Sudan makes its living from growing crops. Many people raise cattle, sheep, camels, or goats. Sheep, camels, and goats are found in the north and west, while cattle tend to be kept in the central and southern regions. A quarter of Sudan's population, some five million people, are nomadic or semi-nomadic, moving from place to place in search of grazing land for their animals. They often grow some crops as well, fitting their movements around the sowing and harvesting seasons.

Both camels and cattle are important exports. They are sent north to Egypt or across the Red Sea to Saudi Arabia and Yemen. As with agriculture, experts estimate that animal production could be greatly increased. And so the government is trying to improve the transport of cattle by rail and to establish watering points along the routes traditionally followed by cattle breeders. Many

A boabab tree. It looks as though it has been planted upside down, with its roots in the air!

tribes still keep only enough cattle to satisfy the needs of their family, or as a status symbol and measure of wealth. In the latter case, they will not part with them except to provide a dowry or bride-price on marriage.

7

Life in the Towns

Before the arrival of the Turco-Egyptians in 1820, there were only four towns of any size in Sudan, each with a population of between six and ten thousand. These were Shendi, Kobbei, Old Sennar, and Suakin. They had originally grown up because they were centers of trade on the caravan routes. Nowadays, Shendi is not particularly important and the other three places are in ruins.

There are still relatively few large towns in Sudan and they are widely scattered. Because these towns are fairly new, most of them follow a similar plan, with a *souk* or market at the center of each district. They are also divided into first, second, and third class residential areas, with separate commercial and industrial zones. Less than 25 percent of the population of Sudan lives in towns. However, more and more people are attracted to them every year, searching for work or for a higher standard of living. Squatter settlements tend to develop on the outskirts. Sometimes the government demolishes these; but some, in time, gain respectability and become part of the town itself.

As this picture shows, at certain times of the year it is possible to see which is the Blue Nile and which is the White Nile.

Khartoum is Africa's hottest capital city. Even in the winter the daytime temperature can reach 100 degrees Fahrenheit (38 degrees Celsius). It is in the northern half of the country at the junction of the Blue and the White Niles. The capital area is often called the Three Towns, as it consists of Omdurman (the original Sudanese capital), Khartoum North (the main industrial area), and Khartoum itself, originally the capital of the foreign powers. Its position at the junction of the two rivers is a significant site for a town. Indeed, the name Khartoum, may well come from a Dinka word meaning "junction of the waters." However, another theory is that Khartoum comes from the Arabic word for "elephant's trunk." Looking down from a plane, the two Niles can be seen to join and then snake off northward as the main Nile.

72

Little is known about Khartoum before Turco-Egyptian times. Then, in 1824, a fort was built there. By the 1880s it was a flourishing town with a palace for the governor general. It was on the steps of this palace that General Gordon was killed by the Mahdi's followers.

After the siege of Khartoum and the Sudanese victory, the foreign capital was abandoned by the Mahdi, who expanded the small town of Omdurman across the river and made it his capital. Although Omdurman had a fine mosque with a large assembly area in front of it, the town consisted mostly of closely-packed modest one-story buildings made of mud brick. This was because the Mahdi and his successor, the Khalifa, saw the town as unimportant in itself. They regarded it merely as a staging post before extending their holy mission to the rest of the Muslim world.

The most impressive building was the Khalifa's house, constructed next to the Mahdi's tomb. It is still standing and has now been turned into a museum containing many relics of the Battle of Omdurman. The Mahdi's tomb, which for Muslims gave Omdurman the status of a holy city, was badly damaged by Kitchener's forces and later demolished. However, an identical tomb was rebuilt in the 1940s and this can be seen today.

After the Battle of Omdurman in 1898, Kitchener turned his back on Omdurman, the Khalifa's capital. A new, modern Khartoum, shaded by banyan and mahogany trees, was built on the other side of the river on the ruins of the earlier Turco-Egyptian town. The focal point of Kitchener's capital was the river front. All the ministerial buildings, as well as Gordon

Memorial College, were built in the early years of the 20th century along the west bank of the Blue Nile, alongside a fine new palace for the governor general. Nowadays, this is called the People's Palace and is used on ceremonial occasions.

In the river between the Three Towns lies Tutti Island, which can only be reached by ferryboat. This is a huge garden market, supplying the town.

Khartoum is in many ways untypical of the rest of Sudan, with 80 percent of all commercial firms, 70 percent of all industry, and 50 percent of all doctors based there. Linked by bridges, the Three Towns, with a population of some two and a half million, form a small, dusty, unhurried capital city.

Juba is the most important town in southern Sudan. It lies to the south of the great Sudd swamp, at the last navigable point upstream on the Nile, not far from the borders with Uganda, the Democratic Republic of the Congo, and Kenya. This part of the country really feels like Africa. The climate is cooler than in the north but more humid, with a definite rainy season. This accounts for the rolling savannah (grassland) which stretches in all directions around the town.

Outside Juba is the first bridge across the Nile since Kosti, some 900 miles (1,400 kilometers) to the north. At this point the river is broad and lazy, fringed with lush mango trees. And it is possible here to glimpse the occasional hippopotamus or crocodile.

Originally, the main town in this area was Gondokoro, famed in the 19th century as a trading post and for its unhealthy climate. Juba is situated on the opposite river bank, a little further down-

A typical street in the town of Juba.

stream. It began to take on importance as an administrative center in the 1930s.

The town is dominated by two huge cathedrals, one Catholic and one Protestant—evidence of earlier missionary activity. There is also a large hospital, an important day school (most schools in the south are boarding schools as students are drawn from villages over a large surrounding area), and a new university on the outskirts.

The electricity supply is often available for only a few hours each day; and oil and gas is in very short supply. The small number of vehicles to be seen are mostly trucks which ply between Sudan and neighboring countries. There are also some bicycles but many people travel on foot.

The dominant tribe in the surrounding area is the Bari but the population of around 120,000 is a mixture of some 30 tribes from all over the south, mostly Nilotic peoples who are tall, slim, and very dark-skinned. So that people can communicate with each other, a common language has evolved, known as Juba Arabic. It is a much simplified form of the spoken Arabic of northern Sudan. Many people, if they have received elementary education, also speak English. Here, clothing consists mainly of simple dresses for the women and shorts for the men, with few tobes and *jallabiyas*.

Nyala, with a population of about 100,000 lies in the savannah zone in the far west of Sudan, in an area known as Darfur ("land of the Fur") near the borders with Chad and the Central African Republic. Darfur, which is about the same size as the United Kingdom, has traditionally been rather isolated from the rest of the country. Indeed, Islam did not gain much ground in the region until the 17th century. It was here that Ali Dinar ruled over his own independent state for 17 years after the beginning of Condominium rule.

However, in 1960, the extension of the railway as far as Nyala connected it more firmly with the rest of the country. Even so, the 800-mile (1,200-kilometer) rail journey from Khartoum (which normally takes four to five days) can, in the rainy season, take up to two weeks! Similarly, during the rains between June and September, Wadi Nyala which runs through the town may flood. Then the town finds itself divided completely in two for some time.

A merchant selling handicrafts in the *souk*.

Because of Nyala's geographical position, a mixture of different peoples and groups live in and pass through it. It is a trade center for imports from and exports to the countries further west in Africa, and also between the settled population and the nomads of the surrounding area. The nomads exchange their animal products for fruit, vegetables, wheat, and millet. Members of the Fur, Birged, Baggara, and Zaghawa tribes live in separate areas of the town. People of West African origin may also be seen in Nyala, as well as northern merchants, the *jellaba* (so called because of their distinctive white robe, the *jallabiya*).

The *souk* (market), like all *souks* in Sudan, is divided into different sections for different products. There are goldsmiths, tailors, ironmongers, second-hand merchants, spice sellers, and so on,

77

Jellaba **(northern merchants) relaxing in the bazaar.**

each in their own separate area. Also on sale will be the handi-crafts of the different tribes, including the distinctive *tabag*–bright-ly-colored woven-straw tray covers—for which Darfur is famous. These keep food hot and free from flies.

Ninety miles (140 kilometers) to the northwest of Nyala is a range of hills of volcanic origin known as Jebel Marra. They rise to a height of over 9,750 feet (3,000 meters). In the heart of the dormant volcano, surrounded by high crater walls, are the Deriba Lakes (known to the Fur as the male and female lakes) and lush pastures where magnificent horses graze. Citrus groves and gar-dens abound here and the new paved road between Zalingi and Nyala has helped development. Since Sudan's economy is basic-ally agricultural, what industry the country has is mainly related to the processing of agricultural products—food, cotton textiles, and leather.

The largest scheme of this kind was the Kenana Sugar Project near Kosti. The sweet-toothed Sudanese love lots of sugar in their tea; the country was importing over 150,000 tons every year. Using western technology and Arab money, land was reclaimed from the desert and machinery imported to form the largest sugar plantation in the world. In 1981, the enormous factory took in its first harvest.

There is also some light industry in Sudan, nearly all of it in Khartoum or Port Sudan. Consumer goods, such as batteries, shoes, and tires, are manufactured and the all-important *souk* trucks assembled.

Potentially, the country is rich in mineral resources, though many areas have not yet been surveyed fully. Even so, some iron ore, gold, manganese, chromite, quartz, copper, asbestos, oil, and natural gas have been found. All industry is dependent upon such things as petroleum, diesel oil, good roads, and a regular supply of electricity. A shortage of all of these, which people in developed countries so often take for granted, means that factories in Sudan operate well below full capacity.

Some hydroelectric power is supplied by dams such as Roseires, Khashm al-Girba, and Sennar, but the Nile River system could be developed to provide more power. At the moment all of the population does not have access to electricity and there are long and frequent powercuts in the hot season when demand is greatest.

The great hope for the future lies in oil, first discovered in

Sudan in 1978. Unless new and greater oilfields remain to be found, there will be only enough for the country's own needs plus a small surplus for export. But even this will have a great effect upon the economy, since about 20 percent of Sudan's current import bill is for oil. Even this amount does not buy enough for all the needs of transportation and industry.

Sudan had hoped to produce 50,000 barrels of oil a day by the end of 1985 and there were plans for a pipeline to carry this from the oilfields to a new oil terminal on the Red Sea. However, until an agreement is reached with the rebels in the south, where the major oilfields lie, production will remain suspended and fuel rationing and shortages for industry will continue.

Sudan also imports manufactured goods, such as textiles, machinery, vehicles, iron, and steel. Because the country imports far more than it exports, it spends more than it earns and has a large national debt that it has fallen behind on repaying. In addition, a decline in the annual rainfall in the past decade has kept

Port Sudan. Across the river is the town's oil terminal.

the agricultural output below average. Sudan is one of the 25 poorest countries in the world, with most of its long-term growth dependent on aid from richer countries.

Historically, too, there has been uneven development in Sudan between the north and the south—the north being more developed. This was the state of affairs when the country became independent and little has been done since to alter the situation. It is another point of dispute between north and south. The south is still suffering from the effects of the disastrous civil war that has gone on for over 30 years.

As Sudan's population is so small compared to its vast size, there are shortages in the workforce which are made worse by the "brain-drain" to the Gulf countries. Anyone who has a skill, from driver to university professor, knows that (with salaries so low in Sudan), he can earn many times more doing the same job in a richer Arab country. Although these people send much-needed foreign currency back to their families in Sudan, it still does not make up for the loss of their skills. Also, as in many developing countries, there is a lack of trained technicians. In practical terms, this means that a developing country often has many engineers but few good mechanics, many doctors but few nurses.

8

Education

The Koranic school, or *khalwa*, is a traditional village institution which has existed in Muslim parts of Sudan since the 14th century. Fifteen to 20,000 of them are maintained (independently of the government) by village communities. Their aim is to teach pupils to memorize at least part of the Koran, the Muslim holy book, and to prepare them for membership of a Muslim society. There is no age limit in these schools, though most pupils are between five and nineteen years, with girls attending only up to the age of about 10. The school, run by a faki, may be a boarding school or it may be more like evening classes, with the pupils seated on the ground under a tree. At the khalwa, as well as memorizing the Koran, pupils also learn to read and write using a wooden slate, again basing their texts on the Koran. In return for the faki's teaching, pupils or their parents do not pay fees; they contribute gifts or labor. The standard method of learning is for each pupil to repeat some verses of the Koran after the faki until the teacher is sure they have been memorized. The faki then passes on to the next pupil while the first one

Dinka primary school children.

continues repeating. With everyone reciting different verses out loud, a khalwa is quite a noisy place!

Many parents today, while proud of this tradition of education, regard the khalwa as rather old-fashioned and prefer to send their children to the government schools.

Apart from the Koranic schools, there are state run schools. In the late 1970s the educational system was reorganized. There is a six-year elementary school program and a three-year secondary school program. After children graduate from this level they can either go on to a three-year college-preparatory school or to a four year school to be trained in commercial arts, agriculture, technical skills, or teaching. In 1975, a national program was set up with the aim of reducing the high (80 percent) illiteracy rate. The idea was that illiterates should study basic reading, writing, and arithmetic for four hours weekly over nine-month period.

They also started an ambitious project, Integrated Rural Education Centers (IRECs) aimed to provide villages with a primary school, childcare clinic, dispensary, skills workshop, agricultural store, and cooperative farm for teaching purposes.

The rural midwife (*daiya*) is a key figure in village society, so it is essential that more and more trained midwives should replace the traditional, untrained ones. Since the first midwifery school opened in Omdurman in 1920, more and more regional schools have been set up. These lay emphasis on simple, practical training, stressing the importance of cleanliness while making use of the everyday objects to be found in even the most modest homes. Midwives are trained to recognize the powders, medicines, and disinfectants they use by feel, taste, and smell. At the end of their course they are issued with a licence to practice, and a basic medical kit, and are encouraged to return to their home areas to work.

In the early years of Anglo-Egyptian rule, the only place in Sudan which offered education above primary level was the Gordon Memorial College. This was set up with money donated by thousands of people in Britain, many of them children, as a permanent memorial to General Gordon in Khartoum. The original buildings of the college, which opened in 1902, stand on the banks of the Blue Nile and form the heart of the present-day University of Khartoum, which has grown up around it.

Later, four other secondary boarding schools were established in the provinces. Many Sudanese in important positions today received their secondary education in one of these four schools.

In 1934, Bakht er Ruda, the first teacher training college in

The beautiful buildings of the University of Khartoum.

Sudan, was set up to train primary-school teachers. It was deliberately built away from the capital, outside the small town of Ed Dueim some 140 miles (220 kilometers) up the White Nile from Khartoum. The idea was that teachers and staff should live in simple conditions while training, concentrating on practical and agricultural skills which they would pass on to their pupils when they returned to rural areas. One significant feature was that Bakht er Ruda's printing press produced textbooks which were used in schools throughout the country.

In 1924, the Kitchener School of Medicine (the first college to offer training above school level) opened. This was later followed by a School of Law and, in 1936, Schools of Agriculture, Veterinary Science, and Engineering. Together they formed the

85

Children at a playgroup.

nucleus of what became, in 1956, the year of independence, the University of Khartoum.

Since independence, education at all levels has expanded enormously. Even though many children still do not go to school at all, there are now over two million children in Sudanese primary schools, compared with under 150,000 in the mid-1950s.

There are three universities in Khartoum and two provincial universities, founded in 1977, at Wad Medani, in the Gezira area, and Juba in the south. Arabic has gradually replaced English as the language of study in the universities.

The government has also tried hard to develop technical education, establishing trade and vocational schools. At a higher level, Khartoum Polytechnic was formed, in 1975, by joining together a number of technical institutes. There are also institutes to train students in such skills as nursing and agriculture.

9

Transportation—River, Rail, and Road

The Nile is the longest river in the world—4,155 miles (6,648 kilometers). The White Nile has its source in Lake Victoria in Uganda while the Blue Nile flows from Lake Tana in Ethiopia. The Nile in Sudan is at present under-used for transportation. To the north of Khartoum a series of six cataracts limit river transport, but the Blue Nile is navigable as far as Roseires, near the Ethiopian border.

On the White Nile, unless fighting in the south prevents it, boats ply between Kosti and Juba, a distance of some 900 miles (1,400 kilometers). This link is especially important as, during the rainy season in the south, land transportation is impossible in many areas.

Because of the Sudd (Arabic for "barrier") which is a huge 2,900-square-mile (7,500-square-kilometer) floating swamp of papyrus and water hyacinth, navigation on this stretch of the river is always tricky. Going upstream from north to south takes a week. Because of the current, the journey takes only four days in the opposite direction. The Sudd teems with birds and wildlife but travelers talk mainly of the monotony of the green water vegetation and the constant harassment of mosquitoes!

Begun in 1978, the Jonglei Canal aimed to drain and bypass part of the swamp, between Bor and Malakal. In addition to making river transportation easier, it would have saved a vast amount of water at present lost through evaporation. The French contractors had enormous technical problems in the construction of the canal, and the activity of southern rebels forced them to suspend digging. The economic benefits of the canal will be enormous, yet some experts wonder what effects the canal will have on climate, on wildlife, and on the traditional lifestyles of the Dinka and other peoples in the area.

There are few bridges across the Nile—only two on the White Nile between Khartoum and Juba. Very often people and vehicles have to cross by ferryboat. Traditional wooden boats are still being made by hand, using very simple tools. These are purchased by merchants and are used to carry goods over short distances.

Sudan's first railway was constructed by Kitchener in the 1890s to transport his invading army. Today there are in all 3,400 miles (5,500 kilometers) of single track which are used by some two million passengers a year. Many of these often have to cling to the roof of the train when they are traveling! Three million tons of freight is also transported. The trains are old and become more

Due to lack of funds, rolling stock has become increasingly old and unreliable. These engines need new parts.

and more unreliable as there is not enough foreign currency to buy new plant and spare parts. But the real enemies of the railway are the rain, heat, dust, and sand. These last three elements mean that the 600-mile (965-kilometer) journey from Wadi Halfa to Khartoum, scheduled to take 30 hours, can take days longer!

Sudan has comparatively few stretches of paved road, for a country which covers almost 1,000,000 square miles (2,500,000 square kilometers). Indeed, it was only in 1970 that the first paved road between Khartoum and Wad Medani—chief town of the Gezira cotton-growing area—was opened. The road has since been extended the full 744 miles (1,000 kilometers) to Port Sudan. Because of this, road transportation has increased in importance,

89

compared with rail and river. Elsewhere, people drive over rough, unmade tracks across the desert or savannah. Of course, for many Sudanese the pace of life is slow and they still get about only on foot or on a donkey.

There is a tremendous variety of road vehicles. The toughest of these, which penetrate to every corner of Sudan, are the *souk* trucks. They carry goods and people between towns and far-flung villages. Often the people are perched precariously on top of the load or are unmercifully bounced up and down at the back. Journeys can last weeks, so the trucks carry food, a large water-skin strapped to their side, sandladders, and several drums of fuel. Sometimes the driver will even take his rope bed along with him! Drivers, who navigate by the sun and stars, often also have to serve as mechanics if the vehicle breaks down in a remote area. In the south, the security situation often prevents trucks from traveling. And fuel is frequently in short supply in both north and south.

Between the main towns there are also inter-city buses, some of them air-conditioned and very modern.

A person has to be quite rich by Sudanese standards to own a car. Fuel is strictly rationed and it is often necessary to stand in line for hours to get it. Most people travel around town using what are called "boxes." These are usually converted pickup trucks with seats for 10 people at the back. They run along a fixed route (indicated by the colored stripes along the side of the vehicle) and charge a small set fare. Passengers have to flag them down from the side of the road, pay the conductor, who is often a

A *souk* (market) truck—these trucks penetrate to every corner of Sudan, carrying people and goods between towns and villages.

young boy, and tap on the metal side when they want to get off. Minibuses and buses also provide public transportation.

One major problem for Sudan is that it has access to the sea only on its northeastern side. This throws a great burden on road and rail transportation. It also means that most of the country's imports and exports pass through Port Sudan, its only sizeable port on the Red Sea, which was constructed early this century. Although much is being done to modernize this port to fit it for containerized shipping, there is often a great backlog of goods into and out of the country.

In northern and central Sudan there were, in the past, a number of ancient trade routes crisscrossing the country. Along these routes traveled vast caravans of up to 2,000 camels. The routes

A camel train. This ancient way of traveling across the desert is still used today (when speed is not the main concern).

changed slightly from time to time to avoid hostile tribes who were only too ready to plunder their rich loads—exports of ivory, gold, ostrich feathers, ebony, and slaves, or imports of salt, cloth, metal weapons, and manufactured goods. Certain towns, such as Shendi, where several caravan routes crossed, became important inland trade centers. The caravan routes were vital in linking the interior to the east coast and to North Africa, especially as the Nile, with its six cataracts between Aswan and Khartoum, was not easily navigable.

Certain routes were also used by pilgrims on their way to Mecca. From the 16th century onward, many West African pilgrims crossed Sudan, often working their way and sometimes taking many years over the journey. Today, their descendants provide much of the agricultural labor force in the cotton-growing Gezira area south of Khartoum and have become a significant element in the population.

10

From Independence into the Future

Sudan began its new, independent life with a parliamentary system of government. It was modeled upon that of Britain with free elections and rival political parties. However, periods of parliamentary rule in Sudan were brought to an end by army officers who claimed they were taking over power to prevent the country from sliding into chaos.

Between 1956 and 1958, and then between 1964 and 1969, there were as many as eight different governments, dominated by the two traditional parties from pre-independence days, the National Unionist Party and the Umma Party. All too often these parties acted only in their own interest, and their rivalry and jealousy led to weak rule. Most of the short-lived governments were coalitions, their ministers chosen from two or more parties with conflicting interests. During this period both the Communist Party and the conservative Muslim Brothers increased in influence and demanded a say in government.

The People's Assembly where Sudan's politicians meet.

As the politicians squabbled, there were two bad cotton harvests, in 1957 and 1958, and world prices for cotton also fell. People were relieved rather than upset when, in November 1958, on the very day parliament was to begin its new session, the army under General Ibrahim Abboud took power.

General Abboud banned all political parties and trade unions and held power for six years, until 1964. During his rule, funding was agreed for the Roseires Dam, which now provides water for irrigation and supplies 50 percent of Sudan's electricity. In addition, a new Nile Waters Agreement was drawn up with Egypt, under the terms of which a High Dam was to be constructed in Aswan.

94

However, opposition to a military government increased. The banned political parties formed a United Front and, together with the Professional Front (formed by doctors, lawyers, and teachers), they forced General Abboud to resign.

The second period of parliamentary rule was even more disorganized than the first—a series of weak coalitions, brought down by votes of "no confidence" in parliament. Dominating everything else was the problem of the civil war in the south. This war had started even before independence and was a constant sore. It divided Sudan, cost a great deal of money, and soured relations with other African countries. For 17 years it was the main cause of unstable government.

In 1955, when preparations were being made for independence, only six government positions (out of some 800) had been given to southerners. People in the south were understandably upset about this. Then, a body of southern troops, who mutinied and later surrendered, were killed by northern soldiers. As news of this spread, many northern Sudanese died at the hands of angry southern mobs.

Government after government tried to crush the southern rebels by force. The rebels, although divided among themselves, developed a well-organized guerrilla army called the *Anya Nya—*"snake venom." The government managed to control only the towns in the south. Some 750,000 southerners fled into the bush and a further 250,000 took refuge over the borders, in Uganda and Zaire. Both the army and the rebels were guilty of appalling massacres. In May 1969, a young army colonel called Jaafar

Jaafar Nimeiri, the army colonel who seized power in 1969 and became president of Sudan until 1985 when he was overthrown.

Nimeiri seized power. As a soldier he realized that there was no way of winning the war in the south, and that peace could only be achieved by talking to the rebels and negotiating with them. Finally, in 1972, on March 3, now National Unity Day in Sudan, the Addis Ababa Peace Agreement was signed.

Once in power, President Nimeiri quickly strengthened his position. In 1970, he attacked Aba Island, a stronghold of the Mahdists who opposed him. He created the Sudan Socialist Union, the only recognized political party. He crushed the Communist Party which had helped him come to power, because it later tried to overthrow him.

During the first 10 years of Nimeiri's rule, the road network in the north was expanded and, for the first time, there was a paved

96

Work on the Jonglei Canal in the south of the country. Construction has been delayed due to civil war in the south.

road between Khartoum and Port Sudan, the country's only port. An oil pipeline was also laid between these two towns, taking pressure off the railway. Money flooded in—much of it from Arab countries—for the development of large-scale agricultural projects such as the Kenana Sugar Scheme. The production of the staple crop *dura* (millet) increased by over 70 percent in five years. In the south, work began on the Jonglei Canal, with the aim of improving communications and irrigation. And enough oil was found for Sudan's own needs.

However, too much happened too fast. In the early 1980s, Sudan fell heavily into debt. In 1973, there had been an 11 million dollar difference between government income and spending. By 1981, this had risen to 800 million dollars!

Although some of the problems the country faced were due to bad management and dishonesty, others were beyond President Nimeiri's control. Money from Arab countries no longer flowed so generously, and the bill for importing petroleum rose dramatically. Then, by 1984, there were over one million refugees who had poured into Sudan from Chad, Ethiopia, and other neighboring countries in order to escape famine, drought, or war.

People became more and more dissatisfied as the cost of living rose by 40 percent each year. Also President Nimeiri made a series of unpopular decisions. He dissolved the separate Southern Region which had been guaranteed by the Addis Ababa Agreement. He introduced his interpretation of *Shari'a* (Islamic Law), with harsh punishments for criminals, such as flogging and the amputation of hands or feet. This angered both non-Muslims in the south and many devout Muslims in the north. As a result, a guerrilla army again became active in the south and work stopped on the Jonglei Canal and the oilfields, both of which are vital to Sudan's economy.

In April 1985, President Nimeiri was in his turn overthrown by the army. General Swaraddahab, the commander-in-chief, promised to hand over power to an elected government after a year and appointed a cabinet composed mainly of civilians. Once again, political parties of all shades of opinion began to function openly. There was political instability for a few years. Then in June 1989 the Revolutionary Command Council (RCC) seized power. It was led by General Bashir. They proceeded to put hundreds of political opponents in jail, banned unions and political

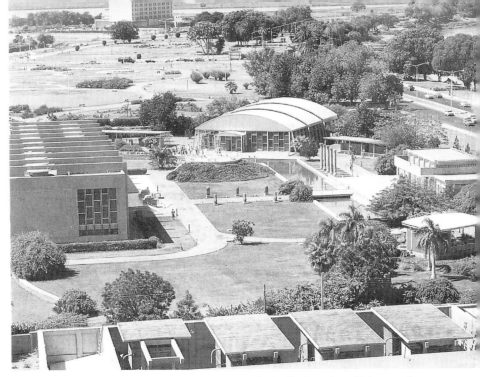

A view from the roof of Friendship Hall, built by the Chinese, in Khartoum—hopefully a symbol of more peaceful times to come.

parties, eliminated the court systems, and closed the newspapers. Through the 1990s the government continued its reign of oppression. It cutoff any aid to the southern regions because of rebel elements there who had been waging the civil war for years. Widespread famine and deplorable living conditions went unaided. But the southern Sudanese People's Liberation Army (SPLA) continued the civil war.

In 1994 the government made a large-scale attack against the southern rebels forcing thousands to flee the country, and thousands of starving and homeless people to be without aid. Some

99

African countries tried to negotiate settlements and in 1997 the Sudanese government agreed to hold a referendum in the south in 2001.

Sudan still faces enormous problems. A settlement must be reached with the rebels in the south so that steamers on the Nile River and *souk* trucks can again link both parts of the country, and so that work can restart on the Jonglei Canal. Once there is peace, drilling for oil (vital for transportation and for electricity generators to provide power for industry and homes) can begin again.

However, agriculture and livestock will remain the backbone of the country and its economy. Every year, the Sudanese will look at the sky as the clouds roll northward and pray for enough rain to grow their crops and to provide water for their animals. Projects such as dairy farms and chicken farms will bring cheaper food products. However, in a country where 80 percent of the people—farmers and herdsmen—still live from the land with little to spare, the real revolution will be on a small, personal scale. It will come from improved seeds and strains of cattle, from better roads and cheaper transportation, so that the small farmer has more to spare and can sell his produce in the towns.

GLOSSARY

cataracts	Waterfalls or steep rapids in a river
evil eye	The belief that someone can take away another person's good fortune by envy
faki	Holy man in the Islamic religion
ghotiya	Circular straw huts with pointed roofs made from stalks
jihad	Holy war in the Islamic religion
Koran	Holy book of the Islamic religion
Ramadan	Holy month of prayer and fasting in the Islamic religion
Shari'a	Code of justice in the Muslim religion
souk	Market place
Sunna	Summary of the behavior and sayings of Mohammed
tabag	Brightly-colored woven straw tray covers used to keep food hot and free from insects
tariga	Religious order of the followers of the holy men in the Islamic religion
zaribas	Fortified trading posts

INDEX

102

9/06, 1